A STUDY *of* JESUS

Surrendered

LEADER GUIDE

Letting Go & Living Like Jesus

BARB ROOSE

Abingdon Women/Nashville

Surrendered
Letting Go and Living Like Jesus
Leader Guide

ISBN 978-1-5018-9630-9

20 21 22 23 24 25 26 27 28 29 — 10 9 8 7 6 5 4 3 2 1
MANUFACTURED IN THE UNITED STATES OF AMERICA

Contents

About the Author 4

Introduction 5

Leader Helps 11

Week 1: Waking Up in the Wilderness 13
      (Matthew 4:1; Mark 1:12-13; Luke 4:1)

Week 2: What Are You Hungry For? 21
      (Matthew 4:2)

Week 3: Letting Go of Circumstances 27
      (Matthew 4:5-7)

Week 4: Letting Go of Expectations 35
      (Matthew 4:8-11)

Week 5: Living Like Jesus 43
      (Matthew 4:11)

Week 6: Blessings of the Surrendered Life 51
      (Isaiah 61:3; Ephesians 3:20; 1 Peter 5:7)

Video Viewer Guide Answers 59

Group Roster 61

About the Author

Barb Roose is a popular speaker and author who is passionate about connecting women to one another and to God, and helping them apply the truths of God's Word to the practical realities and challenges they face as women in today's culture. Barb enjoys teaching and encouraging women at conferences and events across the country, as well as internationally. She is the author of the Bible studies *I'm Waiting, God: Finding Blessing in God's Delays*; *Joshua: Winning the Worry Battle*; and *Beautiful Already: Reclaiming God's Perspective on Beauty* and the books *Winning the Worry Battle: Life Lessons from the Book of Joshua* and *Enough Already: Winning Your Ugly Struggle with Beauty*. She also writes a regular blog at BarbRoose.com and hosts the "Better Together" podcast. Previously Barb was executive director of ministry at CedarCreek Church in Perrysburg, Ohio, where she served on staff for fourteen years and co-led the annual Fabulous Women's Conference that reached more than ten thousand women over five years. Barb is the proud mother of three adult daughters and lives in northwest Ohio.

Follow Barb:

  @barbroose

  @barbroose

  Facebook.com/barbararoose

Blog BarbRoose.com (check here for event dates and booking information)

Introduction

What happens when life doesn't go as planned?

As much as we know that we don't always have control over our life circumstances, there's often this little voice in our mind that whispers, "If you work hard enough, smart enough, and long enough, you can fix this." Have you ever heard that voice? I have. And for a very long time, I believed that philosophy. In fact, there were lots of times when I didn't pray about some problems. Why pray when I didn't think that I needed God's help?

As a Jesus-loving woman, it is hard to acknowledge my control-loving ways, but when I stopped being afraid to let go and trust God with whatever happened in my life, everything changed. I decided to let go and let God carry the weight and work out what would come next.

Whether your tendency, like mine, is to try to control and fix problems, or you're more inclined to try to escape them or beg God to change things, the bottom line is that painful circumstances are *hard*. If a circumstance in your life has you feeling powerless, afraid, desperate, or alone, I'm glad that you're here for this *Surrendered* Bible study. As we journey together for the next six weeks, you'll have the opportunity to apply God's precious promises to the fears deep in your heart as well as learn helpful tools to reshape your attitudes and behaviors into responses that reflect how Jesus responded in difficult circumstances.

As you lead a group of women through this study, you'll follow Jesus into the Judean wilderness where He was tempted by the devil. We'll explore the wilderness as a metaphor for those long seasons of life when we face hardships and difficulties that test and challenge our faith. As we look at how Jesus faces a set of three temptations, we'll compare his responses to the Israelites, who also faced a long wilderness season centuries before. Throughout the study, you'll also explore how the Israelites' lack of faith made their time in the wilderness painful, yet still they experienced God's power and blessing in their lives.

If there was a word that captured Jesus' posture in the wilderness, that word would be *surrender*. As we trace Jesus' footsteps in the wilderness, you'll learn from His words as well as His actions. Whether you and the women in your group are facing a long wilderness season or dealing with difficult or destructive temptations, Jesus understands what you're going through. You are not alone. There's hope! The goal of this study is to equip each of you to begin the process of letting go and giving over whatever you are facing to God and living each day with the faith that God is in control and He is good.

About the Participant Workbook

Before the first session, you will want to distribute copies of the participant workbook to the members of your group. Be sure to communicate that they are to complete the first week of readings *before* your first group session. For each week there is a Scripture memory verse and five readings or lessons that combine study of Scripture with personal reflection and application. On average each lesson can be completed in about twenty to thirty minutes. Completing these readings each week will prepare the women for the discussion and activities of the group session.

About This Leader Guide

As you gather each week with the members of your group, you will have the opportunity to watch a video, discuss and respond to what you're learning, and pray together. You will need access to a television and DVD player with working remotes, or, if you're downloading the video sessions from online, a computer with a screen large enough for the group to watch together.

Creating a warm and inviting atmosphere will help make the women feel welcome. Although optional, you might consider providing snacks and drinks or coffee for your first meeting and inviting group members to rotate in bringing refreshments each week.

This leader guide and the video lessons will be your primary tools for leading each group session. In this book you will find outlines for six group sessions, each formatted for either a 60-minute or 90-minute group session:

60-Minute Format

Leader Prep	(Before the Session)
Welcome and Opening Prayer	2 minutes
Icebreaker	3 minutes
Video	25–30 minutes
Group Discussion	20–25 minutes
Closing Prayer	3–5 minutes

90-Minute Format

Leader Prep	(Before the Session)
Welcome and Opening Prayer	2 minutes
Icebreaker	3 minutes
Video	25–30 minutes
Group Discussion	35 minutes
Deeper Conversation	15 minutes
Closing Prayer	5 minutes

As you can see, the 90-minute format is identical to the 60-minute format but has more time for group discussion plus a Deeper Conversation exercise for small groups. Feel free to adapt or modify either of these formats, as well as the individual segments and activities, in any way to meet the specific needs and preferences of your group.

Here is a brief overview of the elements included in both formats:

Leader Prep (Before the Session)

For your preparation prior to the group session, this section provides an overview of the week's biblical story and theme, the week's Surrender Principle, key Scriptures, and a list of materials and equipment needed. Be sure to review this section, as well as read through the entire session outline, before your group time in order to plan and prepare. If you choose, you also may find it helpful to watch the video lesson in advance.

Welcome and Opening Prayer (2 minutes)

Create a warm, welcoming environment as the women are gathering before the session begins. Consider either lighting one or more candles, providing coffee or other refreshments, or playing worship music, or all of these. (Bring an iPod, smartphone, or tablet and a portable speaker if desired.) Be sure to provide name tags if the women do not know one another or you have new participants in your group. Then, when you are ready to begin, lead the group in prayer before you begin your time.

You also may find it helpful to read aloud the week's overview found in the Leader Prep section if not all group members have completed their homework.

Icebreaker (3 minutes)

Use the icebreaker to briefly engage the women in the topic while helping them feel comfortable with one another.

Video (25–30 minutes)

Next, watch the week's video segment together. Be sure to direct participants to the Video Viewer Guide in the participant workbook, which they may complete as they watch the video. (Answers are provided on page 59 of this guide and page 202 in the participant workbook.)

Group Discussion (20–35 minutes, depending on session length)

After watching the video, choose from the questions provided to facilitate group discussion (questions are provided for both the video segment and the participant workbook material). For the participant workbook portion, you may choose to read aloud the discussion points or express them in your own words; then use one or more of the questions that follow to guide your conversation.

Note that more material is provided than you will have time to include. Before the session, select what you want to cover, putting a check mark beside it in your book. Reflect on each question and make some notes in the margins to share during your discussion time. Page references are provided for those questions that relate to specific questions or activities in the participant workbook. For these questions, invite group members to turn in their books to the pages indicated. Participants will need Bibles in order to look up various supplementary Scriptures.

Depending on the number of women in your group and the level of their participation, you may not have time to cover everything you have selected, and that is okay. Rather than attempting to bulldoze through, follow the Spirit's lead and be open to where the Spirit takes the conversation. Remember that your role is not to have all the answers but to encourage discussion and sharing.

Deeper Conversation (15 minutes)

If your group is meeting for 90 minutes, use this exercise for deeper sharing in small groups, dividing into groups of two or three. This is a time for women to share more intimately and build connections with one another. (Encourage the women to break into different groups each week.) Give a two-minute warning before time is up so that the groups may wrap up their discussion.

Closing Prayer (3–5 minutes, depending on session length)

Close by leading the group in prayer. If you'd like, invite the women to briefly name prayer requests. To get things started, you might share a personal request of your own. As women share their requests, model for the group by writing each request in your participant workbook, indicating that you will remember to pray for them during the week.

As the study progresses, you might encourage members to participate in the Closing Prayer by praying out loud for one another and the requests given. Ask the women to volunteer to pray for specific requests, or have each woman pray for the woman on her right or left. Make sure name tags are visible so that group members do not feel awkward if they do not remember someone's name.

Before You Begin

Friend, my life has taught me that there will always be circumstances out of our control, and the only path to God's power, peace, and provision in the midst of those circumstances is to surrender. I'm so grateful you have chosen to lead a group through this study because I wholeheartedly believe that letting go and living like Jesus will sustain us, strengthen us, and set us up to experience God's best and beautiful blessings, not only in this life, but also in the life to come. Let's get started!

Barb

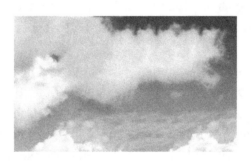

Leader Helps

Preparing for the Sessions

- Decide whether you will use the 60-minute or 90-minute format option. Be sure to communicate dates and times to participants in advance.
- Distribute participant workbooks to all members at least one week before your first session and instruct them to complete the first week's readings. If you have the phone numbers or email addresses of your group members, send out a reminder and a welcome.
- Check out your meeting space before each group session. Make sure the room is ready. Do you have enough chairs? Do you have the equipment and supplies you need? (See the list of materials needed in each session outline.)
- Pray for your group and each group member by name. Ask God to work in the life of every woman in your group.
- Read and complete the week's readings in the participant workbook and review the session outline in the leader guide. Select the discussion points and questions you want to cover and make some notes in the margins to share in your discussion time.

Leading the Sessions

- Personally welcome and greet each woman as she arrives. You might want to have a sign-up list for the women to record their names and contact information.

- At the start of each session, ask the women to turn off or silence their cell phones.
- Always start on time. Honor the time of those who are on time.
- Encourage everyone to participate fully, but don't put anyone on the spot. Be prepared to offer a personal example or answer if no one else responds at first.
- Communicate the importance of completing the weekly readings and participating in group discussion.
- Facilitate but don't dominate. Remember that if you talk most of the time, group members may tend to listen rather than engage. Your task is to encourage conversation and keep the discussion moving.
- If someone monopolizes the conversation, kindly thank her for sharing and ask if anyone else has any insights.
- Try not to interrupt, judge, or minimize anyone's comments or input.
- Remember that you are not expected to be the expert or have all the answers. Acknowledge that all of you are on this journey together, with the Holy Spirit as your leader and guide. If issues or questions arise that you don't feel equipped to handle or answer, talk with the pastor or a staff member at your church.
- Don't rush to fill the silence. If no one speaks right away, it's okay to wait for someone to answer. After a moment, ask, "Would anyone be willing to share?" If no one responds, try asking the question again a different way—or offer a brief response and ask if anyone has anything to add.
- Encourage good discussion, but don't be timid about calling time on a particular question and moving ahead. Part of your responsibility is to keep the group on track. If you decide to spend extra time on a given question or activity, consider skipping or spending less time on another question or activity in order to stay on schedule.
- End on time. If you are running over, give members the opportunity to leave if they need to. Then wrap up as quickly as you can.
- Thank the women for coming and let them know you're looking forward to seeing them next time.
- Be prepared for some women to want to hang out and talk at the end. If you need everyone to leave by a certain time, communicate this at the beginning of the group session. If you are meeting in a church during regularly scheduled activities, be aware of nursery closing times.

Week 1

Waking Up in the Wilderness

(Matthew 4:1; Mark 1:12-13; Luke 4:1)

Leader Prep (Before the Session)

Overview

Throughout this study, we will explore what it means to follow God in the wilderness seasons of our lives. We'll begin our six-week study adventure by following Jesus from a spiritual mountaintop experience in His life—His baptism—into a period of suffering in a stark wilderness, as He is led into the wilderness by the Holy Spirit and then tempted by Satan. Then we'll trail the Israelites as they are freed from their bondage in Egypt and wander and live in the desert, waiting for God to lead them to Canaan, the land God promised to them.

Jesus' forty days in the wilderness mirrors the Israelites' wilderness wandering years. As we study accounts from both the Old and New Testaments, we'll learn not only from Jesus' faithful example but also from some of the missteps that the Israelites made in their struggle to trust God in the wilderness.

We will all face different trials and wilderness seasons in our lives that are out of our control. These seasons are full of fear and doubt and cause us to do everything in our power to try to regain control, but the Lord is calling us to let go, to surrender to Him and His plan for us. He always protects and provides for us.

Surrender Principle #1: I am not in control of others or outcomes.

Key Scriptures

Memory Verse: *Consider it pure joy, my brothers and sisters, whenever you face trials of many kinds, because you know that the testing of your faith produces perseverance.*

(James 1:2-3)

Then Jesus was led by the Spirit into the wilderness to be tempted by the devil.

(Matthew 4:1)

At once the Spirit sent him out into the wilderness, and he was in the wilderness forty days, being tempted by Satan. He was with the wild animals, and angels attended him.

(Mark 1:12-13)

Jesus, full of the Holy Spirit, left the Jordan and was led by the Spirit into the wilderness.

(Luke 4:1)

What You Will Need

- *Surrendered* DVD (or downloads) and a DVD player or computer
- Bible and *Surrendered* participant workbook for reference
- Markerboard or chart paper and markers (optional)
- Stick-on name tags and markers (optional)
- iPod, smartphone, or tablet and portable speaker (optional)
- If you are using the Deeper Conversation option, you may want to give participants index cards or slips of paper to write verses on.

Session Outline

Welcome and Opening Prayer (2 minutes)

In order to create a warm, welcoming environment as the women are gathering before the session begins, consider either lighting one or more candles, providing coffee or other refreshments, or playing worship music, or all of these. (Bring an iPod, smartphone, or tablet and a portable speaker if desired.) Be sure to provide name tags if the women do not know one another or you have new participants in your group. Then, when you are ready to begin, open the group in prayer.

Icebreaker (3 minutes)

Invite the women to share short responses to the following question:

- If you had a magic remote control that could change anything or anyone with just one click, how would you use it?

Video (25–30 minutes)

Play the Week 1 video segment on the DVD. Invite participants to complete the Video Viewer Guide for Week 1 in the participant workbook as they watch (page 47).

Group Discussion (20–35 minutes, depending on session length)

Note: More material is provided than you will have time to include. Before the session, select what you want to cover.

Video Discussion Questions

- How often do we wish we could fix our problems as easily as pressing a button on a remote control? As much as we wish that could happen, we all know that life is complicated and often out of our control. In response, we often exhibit control-loving behaviors in our attempts to handle the situation or relationship. Which of the SHINE behaviors (found in the margin on page 37 of the participant workbook) do you tend to resort to in your life? How does that usually work out?
- Which of the ABCs of surviving the wilderness speaks the most to you right now, and why?
  A – You are *always* loved.
  B – *Believe* that God is for you.
  C – *Challenge* yourself to trust God and let go.
- This week's Surrender Principle is "I am not in control of others or outcomes." Is there a situation in your life in which you need to embrace this principle?

Participant Workbook Discussion Questions

1. In his first public appearance, Jesus goes into the wilderness area where John the Baptist is preaching and asks John to baptize Him. In this moment, it seemed like everything in Jesus' life had come together. He'd taken a faithful step of obedience and experienced the immediate presence and loving affirmation of God. (Day 1)

- Read Matthew 3:13. Imagine yourself in John's shoes, or as someone else who might have been watching that day. What do you imagine it must have been like to witness that moment?
- Spiritual mountaintop moments aren't proof of God's love or favor, but they are memorable moments that remind us of a time when we felt a special connection to God. Can you recall a spiritual mountaintop moment in your life? If you can't think of one, what is a favorite moment in your life? (page 16)

2. No one lives in mountaintop moments, not even Jesus. In fact, right after Jesus is baptized, He experiences a dramatic change in circumstances, as the Holy Spirit leads Jesus out into the wilderness (see Mark 1:12-13). The "wilderness" is a symbol of hardship and difficulty. You may have heard someone refer to a "wilderness season" or a period of time when life is hard or heartbreaking. (Day 1)
   - Read aloud the characteristics of a spiritual wilderness found on page 18 of the participant workbook. Is there or has there been a period in your life that fits the definition of a spiritual wilderness? (page 18)
   - When you're facing a wilderness or hard season, how do you tend to view God?
   - Read aloud this week's Memory Verse, James 1:2-3. What happens to our faith when we experience pressure from challenges and troubles? What is the blessing that comes from being spiritually mature and well developed (or more like Christ)? (page 20)

3. When the Israelites were wandering in the desert and desperately needed food, God sent them manna (Exodus 16:1-4) providing for His people in the midst of their faithlessness, rebellion, and fear. God promises to take care of us, too, but how often do we get anxious because we don't trust God's heart toward us? Jesus addresses this in the Sermon on the Mount. (Day 2)
   - Read aloud Matthew 6:25-32. What are we told not to worry about? (page 23)
   - How can we know that we can trust God? (page 23)
   - Why does Jesus say that worry about tomorrow isn't productive?
   - In your life, how have you seen God taking care of and providing for you? (page 24)

- How does Jesus' teaching challenge your questions about whether or not God will provide for you or a loved one in a challenging situation? (page 24)

4. While there are all kinds of different trials we will face in life, these trials can teach us three important lessons (found on page 30 of the participant workbook): (1) Trials teach us to worship God more. (2) Trials can teach us to depend on ourselves less. (3) Trials can teach us to become more like Christ. (Day 3)
   - As you reflect on these statements, does any of those lessons stand out today? (page 32)
   - Read aloud Proverbs 3:5-6. How much of our hearts should trust God? (page 30) How can we learn to trust God more deeply?

5. Jesus humbly took on our human bodies and limitations (see Philippians 2:5-7) so that we could see how the power of God living within us can help us overcome temptation. It's not a sin to be tempted. We all face temptation, and that temptation can come in all shapes, forms, and sizes. Unfortunately, many of us have been shamed and silenced for feeling tempted. Jesus Himself faced temptation, and He shows us the way to freedom when temptation tries to ensnare us. (Day 4)
   - On page 33 of the participant workbook, temptation is defined as "an invitation that would distract or derail our pursuit of God." How would you define "temptation"?
   - What do Philippians 2:5-7 and Hebrews 4:15 say about why it was necessary for Jesus to experience temptation? (page 34) How does this encourage you?

6. In the participant workbook (pages 36-37) we are given three insights into temptation: (1) Temptation starts with our minds, not our actions. (2) We're often tempted by what we think God won't give us another way. (3) If you've felt a strong pull to fix or have things your own way, there's a spiritual root for that tendency. (Day 4)
   - Which of these insights do you most identify with? How have you experienced these in your own life?
   - Read aloud 1 Corinthians 10:13; James 5:16; and 1 John 1:9. What does each verse say about how God helps us deal with temptation?

7. God called Moses (see Exodus 3) to lead His people in the wilderness; however, Moses struggled with the role that God called him to play. He didn't feel qualified to lead, represent God, or communicate well. Yet the success of God's plan didn't rely on Moses' capacity or capabilities. God proclaimed that it would be His power that would do the work to free the Israelite people. (Day 5)

    *   Read Exodus 3. What were Moses' worries? What obstacles were in his way? How did God answer each of Moses' worries?
    *   In what areas do you struggle with worry and with what ifs? What does Jesus tell us do with our worries in Matthew 6:34?
    *   Refer to the Letting Go Loop graphic on page 44 of the participant workbook. How did working through this exercise help you to see an area in which God is calling you to let go, or surrender control to Him?
    *   Would anyone be willing to share her Declaration of Surrender (page 46)?

Deeper Conversation (15 minutes)

Divide into smaller groups of two to three for deeper conversation. (Encourage the women to break into different groups each week.) If you'd like, before the session, write on a markerboard or chart paper the question(s) you want the groups to discuss. You could also do this in the form of a handout. For the second discussion question below, you may want to give participants index cards or slips of paper to write their chosen verses on. Give a two-minute warning before time is up so that the groups may wrap up their discussion.

*   Is there or has there been a time period in your life that fits the definition of a spiritual wilderness? (page 18) If you are in such a place right now, what are you facing? What is the Lord saying to you?
*   Look up and read aloud the following verses about the promises God has made to us, His children. Which one or more of these promises do you need today? Why? (page 41)

    Deuteronomy 31:8   Psalm 34:17

    Isaiah 43:2   John 8:36

    Revelation 21:4

- Choose one of the verses to focus on and pray over this week. Write your verse on an index card or slip of paper or somewhere else you can display the verse this week and be reminded of God's promise to you in this season of your life.

Closing Prayer (3–5 minutes, depending on session length)

Close the session by taking personal prayer requests from group members and leading the group in prayer. As you progress to later weeks in the study, you might encourage members to participate by praying out loud for one another and the requests given.

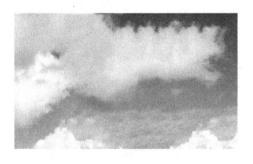

Week 2

What Are You Hungry For?

(Matthew 4:2)

Leader Prep (Before the Session)

Overview

All of us battle a challenging case of the "I wants." This strong feeling captures your desire for a person, place, feeling, or thing, and you can't get it off your mind until you get it. The "I wants" are powerful feelings that we can't always put into words and, if left unmanaged, might cause us to follow those feelings and cause pain or harm to ourselves and others. Just because we love Jesus doesn't mean we don't have to deal with the "I wants."

This week we saw that the Israelites grumbled and complained about what they want, and God responded in a dramatic way. We also observed Jesus as He faced the first of three temptations from Satan—the temptation to believe that we can use God to give us what we want. This temptation resonates hard with us as human beings; however, Jesus teaches us that the invitation in the midst of this temptation is to discover that God is and will always be 100 percent what we need.

Surrender Principle #2: I will live by faith rather than rush to follow my feelings.

Key Scriptures

Memory Verse: *"But seek first his kingdom and his righteousness, and all these things will be given to you as well."*

(Matthew 6:33)

After fasting forty days and forty nights, [Jesus] was hungry.
(Matthew 4:2)

What You Will Need

- *Surrendered* DVD (or downloads) and a DVD player or computer
- Bible and *Surrendered* participant workbook for reference
- Markerboard or chart paper and markers (optional)
- Stick-on name tags and markers (optional)
- iPod, smartphone, or tablet and portable speaker (optional)

Session Outline

Welcome and Opening Prayer (2 minutes)

Welcome the women back to the study and when you are ready to begin, lead the group in prayer.

Icebreaker (3 minutes)

Ask: We see ads all the time for things we "must have." Have you ever seen one of these ads, gotten a serious case of the "I wants," and bought that product or service? What was it, and what happened after?

Video (25–30 minutes)

Play the Week 2 video segment* on the DVD. Invite participants to complete the Video Viewer Guide for Week 2 in the participant workbook as they watch (page 81).

Group Discussion (20–35 minutes, depending on session length)

Note: More material is provided than you will have time to include. Before the session, select what you want to cover.

Video Discussion Questions

- There are times when acting in faith is contrary to how we feel. When have you experienced this in your life?
- Is fasting (from food, shopping, social media, etc.) a part of your life? If so, what motivated you to fast and what happened as a result?
- If we are what we "eat," how does the Lord's command to us in Joshua 1:8 change us?
- Are there any ships in your life that you might need to sink?

Participant Workbook Discussion Questions

1. Jesus chooses to endure His wilderness experience as wholly human, and in doing so, teaches us how to approach our deepest hungers and how to surrender those hungers to the only One who satisfies. (Day 1)
   - Read aloud our memory verse for this week: Matthew 6:33. One of the various definitions of the word *seek* is "crave," and *crave* indicates a strong desire for something. According to Matthew 6:33, what are we to seek (or crave) as followers of Christ? (page 53)
   - What is Jesus' promise to us when we live God's priorities before our own interests? (page 53)
2. In Matthew 4:1-4, the devil came to Jesus, and Satan's first temptation targets Jesus' deepest point of physical weakness: hunger. This reminds me that Satan is going to put pressure on my greatest human need that feels the weakest in the moment. So, wherever you're feeling the most unfulfilled or empty, you're likely to be tempted to satisfy that space. (Day 2)
   - In what areas do you often find yourself tempted? How do you typically respond to that temptation?
   - Remember that Satan typically goes after our weak points, especially when we are tired and worn out and weary. What words or justifications for your behavior do you hear when you are tempted?
3. Notice that Jesus' reply to Satan in Matthew 4:4 begins with "It is written," showing that He was deferring to God's Holy Word rather than voicing His own opinion or rebuttal. Notice how Jesus doesn't argue with Satan; rather, His first move is to elevate the authority

of God's words. Here Jesus is quoting Deuteronomy 8:3, in which Moses is reminding the Israelites about how God had provided for them in all their years of wandering in the wilderness. (Day 2)

- Read Matthew 4:4. What does it mean to live by every word that comes from the mouth of the Lord? (page 57)
- Read Hebrews 4:12. Why do we need the truth of God's Word to cut so deep into our hearts, minds, and souls? (page 58)

4. This week we observed the Israelites in the wilderness and saw what happens when God gives them exactly what they want. At the core of their "I wants" rumbled a dissatisfaction and distrust of God. They believed that if they got what they really wanted, then they would be happy. So God gives it to them in a dramatic way. (Day 3)

- Read Numbers 11:4-6, 31-33. What did the Israelites complain about and wish that they had? (page 60) How did God respond?
- What do the Israelites' complaints say about their deeper desires?
- Can you think of something you've been asking God for but you may not be ready to receive? (page 62) In the past, when have you believed you'd gain happiness by getting something you wanted, only to regret it when you got it?
- In what area of your life do you need to honor God's provision and express more gratitude? Is there a next step or action step that you feel God is prompting you to take today in order to honor Him more in your life? (page 64)

5. Surrender Principle #2 says: "I will live by faith rather than rush to follow my feelings." Our feelings aren't wrong, but unchecked and unchallenged, they can lead us to do wrong things. Our feelings scream "Fix it now!" while faith says, "Trust God's way." (Day 4)

- Are there any emotions that are hard for you to control? How are your reactions to those feelings and emotions affecting you, or those around you?
- What does this surrender principle mean to your life in what you're facing right now? (page 65)

6. As the Israelites move through the desert, we see God physically guiding them in the form of a cloud (see Numbers 9:15-17). The pillar of cloud and the pillar of fire existed to remind the people

that God was with them. It was a visible reminder of His constant presence even though they would continue to struggle to trust God time and time again. (Day 4)

- What kinds of emotions do you think the Israelites might have been experiencing (as they left Egypt and began to travel into the unknown)? (page 68)
- God used an external symbol to guide the Israelites and help them move toward His best for them. Today we have the internal presence of the Holy Spirit dwelling in our hearts to help lead us in our lives. On page 69 of the participant workbook, you were asked to look up Scriptures that give a description or attribute of the Holy Spirit and match them with the correct attribute. Which attribute of the Holy Spirit do you most connect with right now? Why?
- How does the Holy Spirit help you let go and live like Jesus, responding to emotions in a healthy way, rather than follow your feelings into unhealthy or control-loving behaviors? (page 69) Share some examples.

7. As Jesus taught and talked to the hurting, broken, lost, and suffering, He invited them to replace their idols or "pacifiers" with a satisfying connection with Him. The psalmist provides us a visual lesson in Psalm 42:1-2 of what it looks like to come to Jesus and be satisfied: "As the deer pants for streams of water, / so my soul pants for you, my God. / My soul thirsts for God, for the living God." (Day 5)

- How does Psalm 42:1-2 speak to our daily need for God? What image is used here for "satisfaction"? (page 75)
- How does your time with God—whether in Bible study, prayer, worship, or silent meditation—satisfy you? (page 76)
- If you don't feel satisfied after spending time with God in one of these ways, have you identified any of the reasons why? What could make it more satisfying? (page 76)

Deeper Conversation (15 minutes)

Divide into smaller groups of two to three for deeper conversation. (Encourage the women to break into different groups each week.) If you'd like, before the session, write on a markerboard or chart paper the question(s) you want the groups to discuss. You could also do this in the form of a handout. Give a two-minute warning before time is up so that the groups may wrap up their discussion.

- At the end of this week there was an exercise in the participant work-book called "Figure Your Trigger" (pages 76-80). What did the Holy Spirit reveal to you through this exercise?
- Are there any areas in which you could use some accountability in dealing with your triggers? If so, how could this group support and help you? Are there any next steps you need to take?

Closing Prayer (3–5 minutes, depending on session length)

Close the session by taking personal prayer requests from group members and leading the group in prayer. You might encourage members to participate in the Closing Prayer by praying out loud for one another and the requests given.

---

*The reference to Barry Schwartz in the video attributes his ideas to the book *Future Shock*, but the correct book title is *The Paradox of Choice*.

Week 3

Letting Go of Circumstances

(Matthew 4:5-7)

Leader Prep (Before the Session)

Overview

"Letting go" is not something that comes easily for most us. Whether we are facing difficult challenges in our own lives or helping those around us who are in trouble, we are constantly fighting to keep control of our circumstances and make things go the way we want them to.

This week we read about Jesus' second temptation (Matthew 4:5-7), in which Satan challenges Jesus to act outside of God's promises. However, Jesus possessed complete clarity around who He was and what He came to do. That clarity equipped Jesus to avoid testing God and instead trust in God's plans for His life and ministry. This temptation highlights our very human desire to force God to follow our agenda or to assume He will rescue us from any situation we might find ourselves in. But as Jesus shows us, we must lean into and trust God's ultimate plan for us and those whom we care about.

Often our lack of trust comes through when we are afraid and stressed, as in the case of the Israelites. Moses took matters into his own hands and faced the consequences of his reckless actions. Fear and lack of trust in God's promises led the

Israelites to doubt that God could take care of them and fulfill His word to give them the Promised Land.

God can transform our hearts and minds when we learn to open our hands and let go of trying to fix a situation. Seeking His best, even if there is pain and hurt involved, isn't an easy journey, but it's worth it.

Surrender Principle #3: I can always let go and give my problems to God.

Key Scriptures

Memory Verse: [There's] a right time to hold on and another to let go.
(Ecclesiastes 3:6 MSG)

Then the devil took him to the holy city and had him stand on the highest point of the temple. "If you are the Son of God," he said, 'throw yourself down. For it is written:

"'He will command his angels concerning you,
and they will lift you up in their hands,
so that you will not strike your foot against a stone.'"

Jesus answered him, "It is also written: 'Do not put the Lord your God to the test.'"
(Matthew 4:5-7)

What You Will Need

- *Surrendered* DVD (or downloads) and a DVD player or computer
- Bible and *Surrendered* participant workbook for reference
- Markerboard or chart paper and markers (optional)
- Stick-on name tags and markers (optional)
- iPod, smartphone, or tablet and portable speaker (optional)

Session Outline

Welcome and Opening Prayer (2 minutes)

Welcome the women back to the study and when you are ready to begin, open the group in prayer.

Icebreaker (3 minutes)

Ask: This week we have been talking a lot about fear and the effect it has on our lives. Do you have an unusual or irrational fear? If so, share briefly how it has affected your life.

Video (25–30 minutes)

Play the Week 3 video segment on the DVD. Invite participants to complete the Video Viewer Guide for Week 3 in the participant workbook as they watch (page 106).

Group Discussion (20–35 minutes, depending on session length)

Note: More material is provided than you will have time to include. Before the session, select what you want to cover.

Video Discussion Questions

- Have you ever let your frustrations over your circumstances overshadow your faith? If so, what were the circumstances, and what happened?
- Do you tend to see God as someone you can trust with your burdens and worries? Or do you sometimes doubt that provision and try to hold on to it yourself?
- What do you think it means to live in an openhanded posture?

Participant Workbook Discussion Questions

1. This week's study opens with Satan tempting Jesus yet again, this time tempting Jesus to display His power and force God to act. Satan takes Jesus to the highest point of the temple, known as Herod's Temple. As Jesus stands at the top of the temple, Satan proposes that if Jesus jumps off the highest point of the temple, angels would save Him. To back up his pitch, Satan references Scripture and begins his recitation with, "It is written," the same phrase that Jesus used in Matthew 4:4 to overcome the first temptation. Then Satan proceeds to quote Psalm 91:11-12; however, he twists the Scripture to fit his agenda. (Day 1)
   - Read aloud Matthew 4:5-7 and Psalm 91:11-12 and compare the two verses. What phrase does Satan leave out from Psalm 91:11? (page 90)
   - The phrase "to guard you in all your ways" suggests our obedience in submitting to God, no matter the circumstances. Why do you think Satan omitted this phrase?

- It's sobering to realize that Satan also knows the Scriptures. What's helpful to remember is that Satan lies 100 percent of the time, but we must be able to identify his lies. According to Psalm 119:11, how can we prepare ourselves to spot half-truths and lies when we hear them?

2. This week's memory verse is taken from an ancient text written long ago, but its wisdom holds true for us today: "[There's] a right time to hold on and another to let go" (Ecclesiastes 3:6 MSG). Part of our struggle with giving over or surrendering is that we don't often agree with God's time line for how things happen in our lives. While this verse alludes to a "right time," that doesn't always line up with what we'd designate as "our time." (Day 1)

   - Read aloud the following verses and name the promises or reassurances that God gives us about His perfect timing:
     Proverbs 3:5-6
     Jeremiah 29:11-12
     2 Peter 3:8-9

   - Has there been a time in your life when you felt "stuck," waiting for God's timing to work things out? If so, how did you respond, and what happened?

3. In this week's study, we see the Israelites once again losing faith that God would take care of them and do what He said He would do. They go to Moses, who takes the request to God. (Day 2)

   - Read Numbers 20:6-13. What do you imagine was going on in Moses' mind in this situation? (Remember that the people were complaining to Moses *often*.)

   - In the "frustration wilderness," we are easily tempted to seek our own solutions or take credit for God's provision. In doing so, there are spiritual and relational consequences to taking God's plan and doing it our way. What were the consequences of Moses' actions? What do you think about those consequences?

   - Can you identify a time when you knew what God was calling you to do but you decided to do it your way? What happened as a result? (page 91)

- While the Israelites did receive their water, Moses failed to follow God in obedience. He also failed to give God glory for their provision. Instead, Moses tossed out God's plan in favor of an anger-driven reaction to the people's complaining. How do you identify with Moses in this passage? What are or have been some of God's ways or instructions that you've struggled to totally obey or completely surrender to? (page 91)

4. Part of learning to trust God more is learning to control our fears. But we have only to look to the Israelites to see how fear never goes down without a fight! In Numbers 13, the Israelites reach the border of the Promised Land and God tells Moses to send out twelve spies to scout the land. The spies' report was daunting: the land was fertile and beautiful but was controlled by strong and powerful people (vv. 26-33). Only two spies, named Joshua and Caleb, reminded the people of God's faithfulness and promises. Unfortunately, the Israelites were gripped with fear. (Day 3)

   - Read Numbers 14:1-10. How does the people's fear cause them to act?

   - At Moses' request, God forgives the people, but what does He say will be the consequence of the people's actions (found in Numbers 14:29-30)?

   - Has there ever been a time when your fear about something or someone caused you to sin or affected your relationship with God? (page 95)

   - Read 1 John 4:18. What is not a part of love? (page 95) What does this verse tell us about fear, something we all face?

5. The good news for all of us is that fear doesn't have the ultimate say over us. God's power can destroy your strongholds of fear. But how? (Day 3)

   - Read 2 Corinthians 10:5. How do we destroy our wrong thoughts? What does it mean to make our thoughts obedient to Christ? (page 95)

   - Fear tries to convince us that we don't have options, but we do! This week's Surrender Principle is "I can always let go and give my problems to God." How does 1 Peter 5:7 speak to this?

- In Joshua 9, we read a fascinating story about what can happen when we refuse to let go and we end up assuming responsibility for other people's problems. Joshua, the Israelites' new leader, ignores God's instructions about not entering into any treaties with people living in the land of Canaan. He makes a deal with the Gibeonites, and as a result, Joshua and the Israelites ended up being responsible for the Gibeonite people, a new burden of responsibility God never intended for them to carry. The same goes for us. When we try to fix others' lives, we might be successful in certain situations, but we end up carrying the weight of a responsibility not meant for us. (Day 4)
- Have there been times you have wound up rescuing people who should be responsible for their actions or behaviors? In your experience, what has been the personal cost of trying to fix someone else's life? (page 100)
- It's a hard and heartbreaking situation when the people you love or care about are making irresponsible, immature, or dangerous decisions in their lives. However, we must resist reacting with control-loving behaviors in order to save them from necessary consequences. Read Jeremiah 29:11. How does this verse speak to God's provision for those people? How does it speak to God's provision for you?

6. When it comes to practicing letting go and trusting God to guide and to provide, sometimes we need practical tools and techniques to help guide us. (Day 5)
   - Which of the practical tools found on pages 103-105 of the participant workbook is most helpful for where you're struggling to let go? (page 104)
   - What changes or improvements might take place in your relationship if you activated that tool? (page 104)
   - How does James 1:5 encourage you today in this situation?

Deeper Conversation (15 minutes)

Divide into smaller groups of two to three for deeper conversation. (Encourage the women to break into different groups each week.) If you'd like, before the session, write on a markerboard or chart paper the question(s) you want the groups to discuss. You could also do this in the form of a handout. Give a two-minute warning before time is up so that the groups may wrap up their discussion.

- In what areas of your life are you experiencing a stronghold of fear? What encouragement can you draw from Matthew 6:25-34 and Psalm 46:1? (Refer to Day 3, pages 93-94.)
- Read Mark 12:30-31 and summarize Jesus' two commandments for your life. (page 91) How would embracing these commandments—and not adding to them with control-loving behaviors—relieve some of the burdens you are carrying for yourself and for others?

Closing Prayer (3–5 minutes, depending on session length)

Close the session by taking personal prayer requests from group members and leading the group in prayer. Encourage members to participate in the Closing Prayer by praying out loud for one another and the requests given.

Week 4

Letting Go of Expectations

(Matthew 4:8-11)

Leader Prep (Before the Session)

Overview

Any one of us can fall into the trap of self-promotion or pride, whether it's wanting to be praised for leading a particular ministry, using a gift that's publicly recognized such as teaching or singing, or "strutting" because we hold a particular organizational position or job title. We're all susceptible to using for our own gain what others should see as God's glory.

This week in our study, we saw Jesus face Satan's third temptation. Satan offered Jesus the entire world if Jesus would bow down and worship him. The question in this temptation is, *What will you give up in order to be on top?* As we consider Satan's temptation and Jesus' response, our goal is to let go of our expectations of getting what we want and discover that God is and will always be all that we need. We saw this in the life of the Israelites as well, who, as they wandered in the wilderness, struggled to remember that God was all they needed, even when life wasn't meeting their expectations.

This week we explored a variety of areas in which we need to let go of entitlement, insecurity, and people-pleasing—because those things feed our pride or undermine our desire to worship God. We also considered our physical possessions, asking, *What does it cost us when we're spending more time managing our stuff than serving Jesus?*

Surrender Principle #4: Trusting God's promises will bless me, but pushing my plans will stress me.

Key Scriptures

Memory Verse: "What good is it for someone to gain the whole world, yet forfeit their soul?"

(Mark 8:36)

Again, the devil took him to a very high mountain and showed him all the kingdoms of the world and their splendor. "All this I will give you," he said, "if you will bow down and worship me." Jesus said to him, "Away from me, Satan! For it is written: 'Worship the Lord your God, and serve him only.'" Then the devil left him, and angels came and attended him.

(Matthew 4:8-11)

What You Will Need

- *Surrendered* DVD (or downloads) and a DVD player or computer
- Bible and *Surrendered* participant workbook for reference
- Markerboard or chart paper and markers (optional)
- Stick-on name tags and markers (optional)
- iPod, smartphone, or tablet and portable speaker (optional)

Session Outline

Welcome and Opening Prayer (2 minutes)

Welcome the women back to the study and when you are ready to begin, lead the group in prayer.

Icebreaker (3 minutes)

Ask: This week we're talking about expectations. What is one expectation you have for how things should be done in your household or workplace (for example, perhaps about how things are organized or what the daily schedule should be)? Do you find that those expectations are often met? What effect does that particular expectation being met (or not being met) have on you?

Video (25–30 minutes)

Play the Week 4 video segment on the DVD. Invite participants to complete the Video Viewer Guide for Week 4 in the participant workbook as they watch. (page 138)

Group Discussion (20–35 minutes, depending on session length)

Note: More material is provided than you will have time to include. Before the session, select what you want to cover.

Video Discussion Questions

- Have you ever received something you really wanted? How did you feel after? Was it what you hoped for?
- What or who do you tend to "follow"—maybe online, on social media, and so forth? Who or what is influencing you daily and how do they affect your expectations of what your life should be?
- Which practical tool for letting go of expectations most resonates with you?

Participant Workbook Discussion Questions

1. Though we might say that we know the rest of the world isn't here to make us happy or give us what we want, sometimes our expectations about how life should turn out or how people should behave reveal otherwise. The desperation to protect what we love, fix what's broken, or get everyone and everything back on track may blind us at times from seeing that we've put ourselves or our desires at the top of our priorities. As we study Jesus' third temptation by Satan, we see what Satan's priorities are. (Day 1)
   - Read Matthew 4:8-9. What did Satan tell Jesus that he could do for Him? What would Jesus have to do in order to receive it? (page 110)
   - What does this passage reveal about what Satan really wants?
   - The prophet Isaiah wrote about the "morning star," which scholars have interpreted to be a reference to either a political leader or to Satan, who fell from heaven, or both. Read Isaiah 14:12-15. What was Satan's sin that separated him from God?

- This week's memory verse is Mark 8:36: "What good is it for someone to gain the whole world, yet forfeit their soul?" What does this verse mean to you? (page 113)

2. Satan perhaps tempted Jesus with worldly ambition because of the human tendency to seek power and control. Moses demonstrates how to hold a position of authority while giving God the top spot in his life. Scripture calls Moses a humble man (Numbers 12:3). Moses used his strengths to lead; and although he got upset and frustrated at times, Moses knew that being the leader of the Israelites wasn't about him. He knew that his job was to point people toward God. (Day 1)
   - How would you define *humility* in your own words? (page 112)
   - Who are some of your favorite humble people? What do you admire about them? (page 113)
   - Read aloud Philippians 2:1-4. How does this Scripture define what it means to be humble before the Lord?
   - How does humility open the door for God to bless us? (page 112)

3. There's an uncomfortable paradox that we cannot ignore about the spiritual life: when life is hard, that's when it's easier for us to stay close to God; but when life is easy, that's when we struggle to stay close to God. Comfort feels good, but it can frustrate our attempts to focus on faith. In Deuteronomy 6, Moses teaches the people about how to handle the blessings of the Promised Land, and how to remain humble, seeking the Lord's plans over their own. (Day 2)
   - Read aloud Deuteronomy 6:10-12. What did Moses most want the people to remember as they began this new phase of their lives? Why do you think the Lord gave Moses these words?
   - How do you struggle to stay faithful when life seems to be under control? (page 117)
   - This week's Surrender Principle captures the cause and effect of what happens when we focus on God versus when we focus on trying to fix our circumstances: "Trusting God's promises will bless me, but pushing my plans will stress me." How have you found this to be true in your own life?

4. One of the buzzwords in our culture is *entitlement*. Being entitled means we feel we are owed something. In Luke 15, Jesus tells the parable of the prodigal son. He taught this to an audience that included a group of religious leaders who were trapped in an entitlement mentality. Jesus wanted them to discover that God's love, hope, and grace don't belong only to those who think that they deserve it. (Day 3)

    • Read aloud Luke 15:11-32. How did the younger son display an attitude of entitlement? What about the elder son?
    • Which character of this story do you most identify with and why?
    • What does Romans 5:8 say about our place in God's greater story? Where were we and what did He do for us?

5. Entitlement is the combination of three self-seeking behaviors—pride, materialism, and ungratefulness. Thankfully, Scripture teaches us some entitlement-busters to help us refocus our faith on God and His promises to us. (*Direct attention to the board, chart paper, or handout— see below.*) If the recipe for entitlement is pride, materialism, and ungratefulness, then the letting go of entitlement means cultivating the opposite in our lives. (Day 3)

    Note: *Write the following on a markerboard or chart paper, or create a handout to give to each participant.*

Pride (I'm more important than you are)	Generosity (Luke 6:38)
+	+
Materialism (Having and owning is a top priority)	Humility (Philippians 2:3-4)
+	+
Ungratefulness (Why don't I have more?)	Thankfulness (Romans 1:21)
= Entitlement (I'm owed or I should own)	

    • Where do you see entitlement in our families, workplaces, or American culture? Where do you see entitlement lurking around your life, particularly your spiritual life with God? (page 122)

- How does entitlement keep us from fully experiencing God's grace or completely trusting God? (page 123)
- How can practicing generosity, humility, and thankfulness move us from a posture of entitlement to a posture of surrendering to and trusting God?
- Read Philippians 2:3-4. What are some practical ways we can demonstrate humility? (page 123)
- Read Luke 6:38. What is the principle of generosity in this verse? (page 123)
- Read Romans 1:21. What happens when we refuse to give thanks to God for what He has done in our lives? (page 123)

6. People-pleasing can be another control-loving technique to get people to like us so that we can get something from them that we want. Moses' brother, Aaron, ended up engaging in some people-pleasing while Moses was away talking with God. In Moses' absence, the people started to doubt God's presence and they panicked, wanting to revert to old familiar ways in case things didn't work out with God. While Aaron didn't force the people to sin, his actions didn't help them to move toward God; and there were some awful consequences as a result. Perhaps we can relate to his people-pleasing behavior or the "disease to please," as some have called it. (Day 4)
   - Are you are a people-pleaser? (Refer to the line graph on page 126.) Regardless of your score, who in your life do you feel pressured to make happy? (page 127)
   - How can people-pleasing actually function as a form of controlling behavior? (page 127)
   - What does Galatians 1:10 say about how our desire to please others can sometimes hinder our own relationship with God? How have you found this to be true?
   - Read aloud Ephesians 4:15. How does this verse speak to the difference between being a people-pleaser and someone who wants to show unconditional love and serve selflessly? What benefit do we experience as believers when we actually tell people the truth in love? (page 128)

7. Our lives are filled with a lot of stuff—many material possessions that we spend a lot of money buying and a lot of time maintaining. As we've been exploring this week, Satan offered Jesus the entire world if Jesus would bow down and worship him. This prompts us to ask, *What does it cost us when we're spending more time managing our stuff than serving Jesus?* (Day 5)

   • Read aloud Matthew 6:19-20. Does Jesus say that it is a sin to have material possessions? What will eventually happen to everything that we accumulate on this earth? (page 132)

   • Do you tend to live in "just in case" thinking, when you are keeping anything you could possibly need? What are some "just in case" things that you've been holding on to? (page 135) What do you think is the difference between being frugal and responsible with your things and holding on to those things because of fear that you won't have enough?

   • God isn't against us having material possessions. It's not about what we have; it's about why we have it and whether or not we'll allow God to use it or remove it. How does the openhanded surrender position we've been discussing in this study apply to our physical possessions?

8. It's hard to have peace when our hearts and minds are fixated on protecting our possessions, not on our relationship with God. One of the reasons God gave manna each day to the children of Israel in the wilderness was to teach them that everything they had and needed would come from Him. God gave them what they needed when they needed it. The same applies to us. We must remember how generous God is to us. (Day 5)

   • Read aloud 1 Chronicles 29:11. What does this Scripture say belongs to God? (page 135)

   • Read aloud Malachi 3:10-11. What does God say about giving in these verses? What is God's promise when we let go of our resources and give back to Him? (page 136)

   • Philippians 4:19 says, "And my God will meet all your needs according to the riches of his glory in Christ Jesus." How does this verse challenge you to trust God with everything you have?

Deeper Conversation (15 minutes)

Divide into smaller groups of two to three for deeper conversation. (Encourage the women to break into different groups each week.) If you'd like, before the session, write on a markerboard or chart paper the question(s) you want the groups to discuss. You could also do this in the form of a handout. Give a two-minute warning before time is up so that the groups may wrap up their discussion.

- Were you able to practice the Power over People-Pleasing habits this week (Day 4, page 131)? If so, what happened, and how did it affect your relationships?
- Did you take on the Extra Challenge in Day 5 to give away something that made you uncomfortable (page 136)? If so, what was it, and how did the Lord speak to you through that challenge?
- How did the lessons this week help you confront you own expectations for life, and what happens when those expectations are not being met? What has the Lord revealed to you about your heart in this area?

Closing Prayer (3–5 minutes, depending on session length)

Close the session by taking personal prayer requests from group members and leading the group in prayer. Encourage members to participate in the Closing Prayer by praying out loud for one another and the requests given.

Week 5

Living Like Jesus

(Matthew 4:11)

Leader Prep (Before the Session)

Overview

Living like Jesus is the only way for us to experience true hope, peace, and life. Over the past few weeks we've looked at three temptations of Jesus and how He trampled each one with God's Word. Jesus came to earth to show us how to bring God's promises to the most difficult situations in our lives. In the wilderness, Jesus surrendered all, and in doing so shows us how we can overcome in His power.

This week we studied more closely how to live a life of surrender like Jesus. We read about Jesus teaching His disciples how to live a surrendered life. We've seen Him accept help when He needs it. We've watched Him pray to God the Father for strength and courage to fulfill His purpose. We've learned how He calls us to forgive. Last, we leaned in to see Jesus walk through life with the tension of holding both hope and heartache in both hands. And through it all, we found that we can trust God with our whole lives, knowing that our surrender to His will and plan for our lives will be full of blessings and purposes that we can't even imagine.

Surrender Principle #5: When fear tempts me to flee, fix, or force my way, I will choose to stop and pray.

Key Scriptures

Memory Verse: "'Not by might nor by power, but by my Spirit,' says the LORD Almighty."

(Zechariah 4:6)

Then the devil left him, and angels came and attended him.

(Matthew 4:11)

What You Will Need

- *Surrendered* DVD (or downloads) and a DVD player or computer
- Bible and *Surrendered* participant book for reference
- Markerboard or chart paper and markers (optional)
- Stick-on name tags and markers (optional)
- iPod, smartphone, or tablet and portable speaker (optional)

Session Outline

Welcome and Opening Prayer (2 minutes)

Welcome the women back to the study and when you are ready to begin, open the group in prayer.

Icebreaker (3 minutes)

Ask: When you need encouragement or strength, where do you turn? Is there a particular book or Scripture you come back to often? Is there a place you physically go to remember God's promises for you?

Video (25–30 minutes)

Play the Week 5 video segment on the DVD. Invite participants to complete the Video Viewer Guide for Week 5 in the participant workbook as they watch. (page 170)

Group Discussion (20–35 minutes, depending on session length)

Note: More material is provided than you will have time to include. Before the session, select what you want to cover.

Video Discussion Questions

- In what ways have you seen God take something that was intended for harm and change it for the good?
- How have you connected with God in prayer? What practices or habits help you in your prayer life?
- What does it mean to hold hope and heartache in both hands at once?

Participant Workbook Discussion Questions

1. Letting go is a continuous act of faith, and it's not easy. Living like Jesus isn't about being perfect; it is about surrendering our lives and trusting that God knows exactly what He's doing every step of the way. (Day 1)
   - Review the three temptations and triumphs Jesus models for us, found on page 142 of the participant workbook.
   - Which temptation do you face most often?
   - Which triumph gives you encouragement today?
2. We can be encouraged when we reflect on Jesus' triumphs over Satan's temptation. The principles of surrender to God are evident throughout Jesus' ministry, from His time in the wilderness all the way to the cross. In Mark 8 we see Jesus teaching about what it means to live like Him. (Day 1)
   - Read aloud Mark 8:34-37, and then review the three parts of the verse that show us what it means to be a disciple of Jesus. What does each one mean for us practically? Discuss some examples.
   - Consider Jesus' declaration of what it means to be His disciple and to live a life of surrender. What's the hardest part about this for you? Why? (page 144)
3. In Zechariah 4:6, the angel says to the prophet: "'Not by might nor by power, but by my Spirit,' says the LORD Almighty." This is a reminder that while we can put in our best human effort and even accomplish some good things, there are certain things that only God can do or accomplish. (Day 1)
   - How does this week's memory verse apply to a situation that you're facing today? (page 145)
   - In what ways does this verse encourage and strengthen you?

4. Trials or wilderness seasons feel isolating because it's really hard to explain what you're feeling or going through. But you aren't meant to go through the wilderness season alone. Even Jesus didn't do it alone! After Satan left, Jesus accepted and embraced the help of ministering angels (Matthew 4:11). Too often we struggle to acknowledge our need for help or to accept help when it is freely offered. (Day 2)

    •   How hard is it for you to ask for help or accept help when it is offered? (page 147)
    •   When you offer help to someone, do you sometimes silently judge or criticize them for not having the strength or being too tired to do it for themselves? How does this speak to your attitude about accepting help from others? (page 148)
    •   Read aloud Hebrews 3:13. We are all susceptible to pride, which can so easily harden our hearts and cause us to reject help from others. What are your thoughts about accepting help or support when it is offered to you? (page 148) Why do you think it's important for believers to learn to accept help and encouragement from other believers? What might God want to teach us through that?
    •   What are some of your favorite ways to serve others?

5. Living like Jesus means praying and talking to God on a regular basis. Throughout Scripture we see Jesus getting away by Himself to stop and pray. What would Jesus need to pray about? This week we studied three reasons Jesus prayed: for connection to God, for preparation and gratitude, and in order to live out His purpose. (Day 3)

    •   Jesus prayed because He wanted to stay connected to God. How connected to God do you feel when you pray? What are some of the difficulties or distractions, either around you or in your mind, that keep you from connecting to God in prayer? (page 153)
    •   Jesus prayed before key moments in his ministry as well as before making decisions (preparation). Read aloud James 1:5. What is the benefit of taking time to pray before tackling a problem or considering an opportunity? (page 154)

- Jesus lived in a state of gratitude, meaning that He was thankful at all times, not just when life was going His way. How does giving thanks help you keep perspective while you're dealing with a problem?

- Jesus came to earth to seek and save the lost. Yet, as a human being, He struggled with what surrender would cost him; so He prayed to God for help and strength to live out His purpose. Jesus knew that the cost of surrender would be His life. Read aloud Matthew 26:39. What words or phrases did Jesus use in His prayer to affirm that He was willing do what God sent Him to do? (page 156)

- Jesus didn't pray because He wanted God to do His will. Jesus prayed so that He stayed in step with God's will. He knew that the cost of surrender would be His life. Surrender feels scary if we're only looking at what we might lose. But that is when we most need to stop and pray. This brings us to Surrender Principle #5: When fear tempts me to flee, fix, or force my way, I will choose to stop and pray. (Day 3)

- How can embracing today's surrender principle change a situation you are dealing with today?

- Read aloud Philippians 4:6-7. What template does this give us for living in surrender to God?

6. Forgiveness is a key part of what it means to follow God in all of His ways. In a powerful lesson recorded in the New Testament, Jesus speaks to all of us about the power of forgiveness, even for those who might not seem to deserve it. (Day 4)

   - Read aloud Luke 7:36-50 and discuss the following:
     ◊ How was the woman described? What did the woman do when she showed up at the home where Jesus was eating? (page 159)
     ◊ How does Simon the Pharisee react to the woman's actions?
     ◊ What is Jesus' main point to Simon in verse 47? (page 160) How do Jesus' words speak to the forgiveness that has been extended to each of us?

- Read aloud Colossians 3:13-14. Forgiveness might not make us *feel* better about how someone has wronged us, but in forgiving we experience the blessing that comes with being obedient to what God has called us to do. How have you seen forgiveness transform your life or a relationship with someone else? If you struggle with forgiveness, what do you think is holding you back?

  Note: *It is important to acknowledge that, if a crime has been committed against someone and the authorities should be involved, we must not let anyone shame or guilt us out of reporting the crime. If you sense that any of your members are struggling with a situation such as this, you may want to speak with them privately and invite a pastor or counselor to join you.*

7. One of the lessons we learn in living like Jesus is how to live with the tension of accepting that life is never going to be exactly how we want it to be while living each day full of hope and joy. Jesus knew how to live with the tension of holding hope and heartache in both hands. He saw the depravity of our sinful world along with our pain and suffering, yet He also proclaimed hope and peace for all who want to step out in faith and trust Him. (Day 5)

   - Read aloud John 14:27. What is the message that Jesus gives to His disciples about what they would encounter in life and the perspective that they must hold on to? (page 164)

   - Read Philippians 4:7. How is the peace that God provides described here? (page 165)

   - Can you think of an example of holding both hope and heartache in your life? (page 165)

   - What is at risk if we believe that we can only experience peace when life is good? (page 166)

   - Read aloud Romans 8:18-25. According to this verse, what are the things that we can have hope for in the future? (page 167)

     (Note: *You may want to write these phrases on a markerboard or chart paper as you read to reinforce where our hope lies.*)

Deeper Conversation (15 minutes)

Divide into smaller groups of two to three for deeper conversation. (Encourage the women to break into different groups each week.) If you'd like, before the session, write on a markerboard or chart paper the question(s) you want the groups to discuss. You could also do this in the form of a handout. Give a two-minute warning before time is up so that the groups may wrap up their discussion.

- In what ways have you seen your weaknesses make you strong in God's power? (page 169)
- If you were able to practice Barb's ACTS or CALM prayer tools (found on pages 157-158 of the participant workbook), how did doing so affect your prayer time? Did you hear God's voice in a new way?
- Spend some time together in prayer, practicing using the ACTS tool.

Closing Prayer (3–5 minutes, depending on session length)

Close the session by taking personal prayer requests from group members and leading the group in prayer. Encourage members to participate in the closing prayer by praying out loud for one another and the requests given.

Week 6

Blessings of the Surrendered Life

(Isaiah 61:3; Ephesians 3:20;
1 Peter 5:7)

Leader Prep (Before the Session)

Overview

This week as we've wrapped up our study, we've considered the blessings of the surrendered life—the blessings of redemption, supernatural provision, divine protection, and peace. God is able to take the broken pieces of our lives and bring beauty from them. No matter if you're in a wilderness season, experiencing a difficult trial, or trying to heal from the past, you can give God the broken pieces and trust that He won't leave you broken but will hold you together with Himself. As we've read about God walking with the Israelites in the desert, protecting and providing for them even as they faced danger and prepared to enter into the Promised Land, we've been reminded that God can and will do more than we could ever ask or imagine on our own!

Surrender Principle # 6: Surrender is my only path to God's peace, power, and provision.

Key Scriptures

Memory Verse: *He fills my life with good things.*
(Psalm 103:5 NLT)

Cast all your anxiety on him because he cares for you.
(1 Peter 5:7)

> *...and provide for those who grieve in Zion—*
> *to bestow on them a crown of beauty*
>   *instead of ashes,*
> *the oil of joy*
>   *instead of mourning,*
> *and a garment of praise*
>   *instead of a spirit of despair.*
> *They will be called oaks of righteousness,*
>   *a planting of the* LORD
>   *for the display of his splendor.*

(Isaiah 61:3)

Now to him who is able to do immeasurably more than all we ask or imagine, according to his power that is at work within us.
(Ephesians 3:20)

"The LORD *your God has blessed you in everything you have done. He has watched your every step through this great wilderness. During these forty years, the* LORD *your God has been with you, and you have lacked nothing."*
(Deuteronomy 2:7 NLT)

What You Will Need

- *Surrendered* DVD (or downloads) and a DVD player or computer
- Bible and *Surrendered* participant workbook for reference
- Markerboard or chart paper and markers (optional)
- Stick-on name tags and markers (optional)
- iPod, smartphone, or tablet and portable speaker (optional)

Session Outline

Welcome and Opening Prayer (2 minutes)

Welcome the women back to the study and when you are ready to begin, lead the group in prayer.

Icebreaker (3 minutes)

Invite each woman to complete this sentence: "I am here today because God did _____ for me." Or, invite each woman to share a God-sized dream.

Video (25–30 minutes)

Play the Week 6 video segment on the DVD. Invite participants to complete the Video Viewer Guide for Week 6 in the participant workbook as they watch (page 201).

Group Discussion (20–35 minutes, depending on session length)

Note: More material is provided than you will have time to include. Before the session, select what you want to cover.

Video Discussion Questions

- What are the tangible characteristics of a surrendered life?
- Why is it important to remember that the surrendered life is not about perfection? How does the art form of *kintsukuroi* so beautifully illustrate this point?
- Have you ever met someone who was truly surrendered to God? What is that person's presence like?

Participant Workbook Discussion Questions

1. Although living the surrendered life asks us to open our hands to receive the beautiful blessings that God wants to give us, we still grapple with what to do with pieces of our lives that are changed, transformed, or perhaps missing from who we were before. Rather than defining ourselves by our brokenness, beautiful things happen when we surrender the broken pieces of our lives to God and let Him do His work. (Day 1)
   - Review the illustration and principle of *kintsukuroi* (kint-su-ku-roy) found on pages 174 and 177 of the participant workbook. What emotions does this illustration evoke in you? (Note: *If possible, find a picture of a piece of kintsukuroi pottery and show it to the group.*)

- How have you seen God put something broken back together, either more beautiful or stronger, or both, than it was before? How does this kind of restoration give Him glory?
- This week's memory verse is Psalm 103:5 (NLT): "He fills my life with good things." How would you describe the "good things" that God has filled your life with? (page 178)

2. As we move through our wilderness seasons, we grow in courage, strength, perseverance, and faith, and we realize the increase in the power of God at work in us. This means that we can have the expectation that God will do even more. (Day 1)
   - Read aloud 1 Peter 1:7. Why does God allow His people to go through tests that feel like fire? What is it about gold that is so desirable or attractive? (page 175)
   - Hard times don't last forever! Read aloud Isaiah 61:3. What does God exchange our hardship and heartache for when we trust Him? (page 175)
   - Read aloud Ephesians 3:16-20, going around the group with each person reading one verse at a time. Which part of this passage gives you the most hope or encouragement?

3. Throughout this study we've looked at several stories of the Israelites' forty years of wandering in the wilderness. In the pages of Scripture, there are multiple supernatural stories of how God took care of them as they had to learn how to be faithful to God. As the Israelites prepared to enter the Promised Land, Moses recapped their time in the wilderness and reminded them of the following: "For the LORD your God has blessed you in everything that you have done. He has watched your every step through this great wilderness. During these forty years, the LORD your God has been with you, and you have lacked nothing" (Deuteronomy 2:7 NLT). Moses' words reflect an important truth for all of us: *God will be faithful to us, even when we aren't faithful to Him.* (Day 2)
   - When is a time that God was faithful to you, no matter how big or small the situation?

- Part of living the surrendered life is that once we pull back on our control-loving tendencies, we get to see God's work in our lives more clearly. As we've gone through this study, how have you seen this to be true in your own life?

4. This week we read two stories from Scripture that illustrate for us how God is the Great Provider, and how He can supernaturally provide more than we could ever hope or imagine. We saw Jesus feed a crowd of five thousand (Mark 6:34-37) and God, through Elijah, provide for a desperate widow and her son (1 Kings 7:7-24). These two stories show us that though God may take care of our needs in unexpected ways, He is always there for us, ready to provide. (Day 2)

   - As you reflect on how Jesus took so little and God used it to supernaturally provide for thousands, what does this speak to you about whatever you are worried about today? (page 180)
   - Read aloud Psalm 37:25 and James 1:17. What do these verses tell us about God's provision? (page 182) How can knowing and trusting this change your outlook?
   - Imagine for a moment that you have complete trust that God is going to provide what you need in whatever situation you may be worrying about or trying to fix. What would that feel like? (page 182)

5. It is natural for fear to creep in and hold us back from fulfilling the plans God has for us. Part of living the surrendered life is trusting God through that fear and acknowledging His continued presence in our lives. Like the pillar of fire for the Israelites, God's guidance is the best protection that we have in the wilderness season. However, if we define God's protection as simply *staying safe*, we may circle the wagons and live in fear, missing out on serving others. (Day 3)

   - Have you ever turned down an opportunity to serve others because you were afraid of the risk involved? (page 185) How can a "be safe" mentality hold us back from serving God and others?
   - Read aloud Psalm 119:105. How is God's Word described? (page 187)
   - Just as a lamp casts just enough light in a room to see by, God often guides us with what we need to know when we need to know it. Like the Israelites, who had to rely on God because they didn't know where they were ultimately going, so we are called to rely on God's

leading as we walk in our day-to-day lives. Has there been a time in your life when you followed God, even though you didn't know where it would lead? What happened?

- Psalm 91:14-16 reminds us of God's promises for us in our wildernesses, and throughout our lives. Which of the promises listed in this passage is most comforting or encouraging to you? Why?

6. How do we live surrendered like Jesus when there's still life to be lived and situations to be handled? Matthew 5 records Jesus' Sermon on the Mount, in which He teaches us how to live with godly attitude and character. *The Message* translation of this section of Scripture rings with so many reminders of what it looks like to live the surrendered life and the blessings of peace with God that we experience along the way. (Day 4)

- Refer to the exercise in Day 4 where you interacted with Matthew 5:3-11 from *The Message* translation. Which "letting go" lesson stands out to you the most? Why? (page 191)

- This week's Surrender Principle #6 is: Surrender is my only path to God's peace, power, and provision. How have you found this to be true in your life?

7. At the end of the Israelites' journey, Moses gathered the people one final time to help them remember God's goodness toward them and how they could continue to experience God's goodness in their new land. (Day 5)

- As we wrap up our study, let's read aloud Deuteronomy 8:3-11 and reflect on the journey we've taken here together. (Note: *You may want to go around and have each member read a verse at a time.*)

- Verse 3 begins "He humbled you." When and how has God humbled you, when you realized that you didn't have the kind of control/power that you thought you had? (page 197)

- Think of a time of hardship or trial. When have you experienced God's supernatural provision? (page 197)

- Moses says that God teaches His children like a father disciplines his son (v. 5). What are some discipline/teaching moments that you remember from your own wilderness seasons? (page 197)

- Verse 6 discusses obedience, and Moses frames the reason for obedience so that the Israelites can enjoy the blessings that God has waiting for them (vv. 7-9). Can you think of some areas of your life where you're walking in more obedience to God now than you were before this study? If so, what are they? (page 197)
- Read Philippians 1:6. How long will God keep working on us? (page 193) What encouragement do you draw from this verse?

Deeper Conversation (15 minutes)

Divide into smaller groups of two to three for deeper conversation. (Encourage the women to break into different groups each week.) If you'd like, before the session, write on a markerboard or chart paper the question(s) you want the groups to discuss. You could also do this in the form of a handout. Give a two-minute warning before time is up so that the groups may wrap up their discussion.

- Discuss your experience with the "Creating Your Spiritual *Kintsukuroi*" exercise (page 177 of the participant workbook). How did this exercise deepen your understanding of what God may be doing in the broken places of your life?
- Is there an opportunity or "divine assignment" that you may need to say yes to today? If so, what fears do you need to surrender to God? What is a first step you can take to dive into that assignment? (page 189)
- If you are in, or have recently been in, a wilderness season, how has God used this study in your life? What aspect of living a surrendered life has resonated with you the most?

Closing Prayer (3–5 minutes, depending on session length)

Close the session by taking personal prayer requests from group members and leading the group in prayer. If you'd like, pray the following prayer aloud as you close this study.

God, thank You for walking with us through this experience. Whatever changes we have seen in our lives, I praise You for them! I pray that in the days ahead, we will continue to let go and live like Jesus in everything we say and do.

When tempted to keep score, I pray that You remind us to give grace.

When tempted to helicopter or micromanage, I pray that You remind us to trust.

When tempted to interrupt others or not respect their boundaries, I pray that You remind us to be humble.

When tempted to nag or offer unsolicited advice, I pray that You remind us to be wise and loving with our words.

When tempted to excessively plan, I pray that You remind us to trust in your provision and not to worry about the future.

Most of all, God, I pray we grab on to and never let go of Your enduring, faithful promises for our lives and those we love. Amen.

Video Viewer Guide Answers

Week 1
Scorekeeping
Helicoptering
Interrupting
Nagging
Excessive Planning
always
Believe
all / hard
Challenge
others / outcomes

Week 2
faith / feelings
priorities / plans
Jesus / satisfy

Week 3
truth / lies
timeline
let go

Week 4
happiness / God
worshiping God / eternal impact
personally
Hula-Hoop
think
bless / stress

Week 5
Pray(ing)
Forgiving
hope / heartache
stop / pray

Week 6
power / peace / provision
heart
mind
hands
perfection
holds / together
glory
goodness

Group Roster

Name	Phone	Email

CPSIA information can be obtained
at www.ICGtesting.com
Printed in the USA
LVHW102015270220
648443LV00003B/3